THE
TRUTH
ABOUT
LIES

THE
TRUTH
ABOUT
LIES

WHY JESUS IS MORE
RELEVANT THAN YOU THINK

J. MACK STILES

10 Publishing
a division of 10ofthose.com

DEDICATION

*Dedicated to John T. Lovett,
who heard the word—which changed his
life—to accept the counsel of God.*

British Library Cataloguing in Publication Data
A record for this book is available from the British Library

ISBN: 978-1-914966-57-6

Designed by Pete Barnsley (CreativeHoot.com)

Printed in Denmark

10Publishing, a division of 10ofthose.com
Unit C, Tomlinson Road, Leyland, PR25 2DY, England

Email: info@10ofthose.com
Website: www.10ofthose.com

1 3 5 7 10 8 6 4 2

CONTENTS

The Biggest Lie | 1

Lie 1
I Don't Matter to God | 5

Lie 2
Being Good Is Good Enough | 13

Lie 3
Jesus Is an Inspiration | 23

Lie 4
I've Got to Look Out for Number One | 31

Lie 5
I've Got My Truth, You've Got Yours | 41

Lie 6
Death Is the End | 49

Lie 7
Everyone Goes to Heaven | 57

Lie 8
I Can't Change | 65

Walking in the Truth | 75

THE BIGGEST LIE

I am trying to change your mind.

Perhaps you knew that when you picked up this book. But I want to be completely transparent.

There's a sea of subliminal messages out there, all created by artificial intelligence in back rooms of tech companies designed to keep you unaware of their persuasions. It's the deal we make and, for the most part, we're okay with it. It's fine when it comes to clicking on a video or buying some shampoo, but it's not how we should treat the big questions in life.

And I am trying to persuade you about something far more significant than soap. I want to persuade you that Jesus is who he said he was and that he has enormous relevance to your life.

That's this book in a nutshell.

Jesus is relevant.

A little over two thousand years ago, a man stepped off a small fishing boat and onto a stony beach. There was nothing impressive about the way he looked. A carpenter by trade, he likely had strong, calloused hands and forearms tanned by the middle-eastern sun. He worked with his father. He lived near his siblings. He came from a parochial part of the country, a small settlement tucked away in the north, far away from the celebrity and politics of the capital.

And yet, when *this* man stepped out of the boat and onto the beach hundreds of people crowded round him. They jostled and shouted. They asked questions and wanted to get his attention. Neighbors and friends swapped rumors about him and the impossible things he did—stories of healing sickness with a few words and giving sight to the blind. Someone said he could change the weather. Others recounted his clashes with the religious leaders and his ability to hold an audience for hours. And everyone, it seemed, wanted a piece of the action.

In all the chaos, a father stumbled through. Jairus was desperate. His twelve-year-old daughter—his only daughter—was sick. She was about to die. Jairus was a leader of the local synagogue. Religious. Upright. Respected in the community. He'd tried everything to help his daughter and nothing had worked.

But there was something about this carpenter. Deep down Jairus knew, he *knew*, this man was the only one who could help. As he pushed his way through the crowd, forcing others back, he raised his hand and shouted.

Making it to the front he fell down at the man's feet, wet sand soaking through his clothes.

Jesus stopped.

You may know stories about Jesus. You may not. You might think they are something for religious people. People who are into "that kind of thing." For *those* people, the stories are interesting—maybe. But for you, right now, in the twenty-first century, well, it's just not immediately obvious what these events, what *this* man, has to do with you.

A lot has happened since Jesus walked the earth, but people are still people. Seeking meaning and hope. Struggling with money, and worry, and grief. Smiling over successes and kicking themselves over failures. Feeling shame. Feeling elation. Searching for answers. Believing lies.

Jesus hasn't changed either, nor has his availability to meet with every person, including you.

Each chapter in this book focuses on an individual encountering Jesus from the New Testament. During each interaction Jesus exposes a lie that many of us have been brought up to believe as self-evident truth. Every exposé contains a common thread: The truth is more relevant to you than feels comfortable.

The encounters all come from one of four Bible books: Matthew, Mark, Luke, or John. These accounts are biographies recording Jesus' time on earth—the same story captured from four unique perspectives. And what they show runs to the heart of what it means to be human. For you. For me. Jesus meets our greatest need.

We begin with Jairus, the desperate father on the stony beach.

LIE 1

I DON'T MATTER TO GOD

Jairus begged Jesus to come and heal his dying daughter. So, Jesus followed the distressed man through the winding Palestinian streets to his home; the crowds pressed in, eager to see Jesus and watch what he might do for the sick girl.

There were always crowds around Jesus, too many people for him to care about personally, right? One woman thought so as Jesus and Jairus hurried past:

> Jesus went with him [Jairus]. A large crowd followed and pressed around him. And a woman was there who had been subject to bleeding for twelve years. She had suffered a great deal under the care of many doctors and had spent all she had, yet instead of getting better she grew worse. When she heard about Jesus, she came up behind him in the crowd and touched his cloak, because she thought, "If I just touch his clothes, I will be healed." (Mark 5:24–28)

This desperate woman had suffered under the "care" of her first-century doctors for over a decade. We can only imagine what they were prescribing for her constant hemorrhaging. But, whatever it was, it wasn't working. It was making her a whole lot sicker and a whole lot poorer. And all the while she was isolated from her community. With her condition, she wouldn't have been considered "clean."

No wonder she didn't want to be noticed. She didn't think she mattered enough to Jesus to try and attract his attention. He was busy with other more important things, not least going to help Jairus's sick daughter. She only wanted anonymous healing and to slip away in secret. But that's not how Jesus does things:

> Immediately her bleeding stopped and she felt in her body that she was freed from her suffering. At once Jesus realized that power had gone out from him. He turned around in the crowd and asked, "Who touched my clothes?"
>
> "You see the people crowding against you," his disciples answered, "and yet you can ask, 'Who touched me?'" But Jesus kept looking around to see who had done it. Then the woman, knowing what had happened to her, came and fell at his feet and, trembling with fear, told him the whole truth. (Mark 5:29–33)

Jesus wouldn't let her dissolve back into the crowd. He wanted a face to face with her. Those watching could see her shaking as she fell to the ground in front of Jesus, terrified to see his reaction to her.

Just Another Face in the Crowd?

If you came face to face with Jesus, what do you imagine his reaction to you would be? Would he shake his head disapprovingly? Would he welcome you with open arms? Perhaps he would start encouraging you to try harder? Would he want to be your buddy? Maybe he's so horrified by your life, he would walk away in disgust? Perhaps he would barely notice you, having more important things to do?

Despite the rush to get to Jairus's daughter, Jesus cared enough to stop and seek out the woman who thought he wouldn't have time for her. As she bowed, trembling at his feet, his words cut through the lie:

> He said to her, "Daughter, your faith has healed you. Go in peace and be freed from your suffering." (Mark 5:34)

Others had shunned her, exploited her, and failed her. Yet, Jesus shows God's heart toward this broken woman. He calls her "Daughter," grants her peace, and restores her.

Read through Mark's Gospel and you'll see this isn't an isolated case. Every single person mattered this much to Jesus. He had time for everyone, the rich, the poor, those shunned by society, and those popular and respected. He had time for the important Jairus and for the unnamed woman.

Jesus sees each individual as they are meant to be. He does the same for you. Jesus doesn't rate your value based on your looks, how much is in your bank account, your lineage, or your lifestyle. It doesn't matter if your self-esteem is sky-high or so low it doesn't register on the chart.

However you feel about yourself, Jesus shows us that "I don't matter to God" is a lie.

The Truth: You Matter to God Because...

... He Made You

Our first ancestors were made perfectly by God. In the very first book of the Bible, we read how God created Adam and Eve in his image (Genesis 1:27). In each person you meet, and in yourself, you can see echoes or reflections of God's character. Those characteristics appear in people in multiple ways, but two come to mind.

First, we have the capacity to be self-aware; that is, we have a conscience. Science twists itself into knots, trying to understand how protoplasm and calcium come together to be able to think and know *that* we're thinking.

Secondly, we reflect God's heart of love; the Bible says God is love (1 John 4:16). To truly love is one of the most amazing things about being human.

Bearing the image of God means that all descendants of Adam and Eve have these marks of the divine in them.

That's why everyone from every corner of the globe has value, worth, and dignity—including a panicked father and a bleeding woman. Anyone being true to the Christian faith will value all people.

Jesus sees the inherent value in all people, including you. And what Jesus thinks about you is far more crucial than what you feel about yourself.

You matter to God because he made you. He made you with a purpose.

... He Made You to Know Him

I have a famous friend named Wesley Korir. He's a marathon runner who has won the Boston marathon and the LA marathon twice. He even ran in the Olympics for Kenya.

I suspect he has fans who know more about him than I do. But if those fans saw him in the street, Wesley would walk straight past them unless they asked him for his autograph. On the other hand, if Wesley happened to run into me on the street, he would shout out to me and hug me. Many people know *of* Wesley. They know *about* him. I know him.

God made everything in creation but only humans were made to know God in a living, dynamic, two-way relationship. We were made to "walk with God" (Genesis 3:8), not just to get things from him and slip away like the woman in the crowd. Jesus wants that personal meeting with all who come to him in faith.

... He Made You To Know Him As Father

Every culture I've lived in has an endearing word for father: Daddy in English, *Papa* in Spanish, and *Baba* in Swahili, Kurdish, and Arabic. Often it's the first word a baby will learn. In Aramaic, the language of Jesus, it's *Abba*. When the disciples ask Jesus, "teach us to pray," Jesus goes right ahead and invites them to call God "Father" (Luke 11:1–2).

Many in the world have bad fathers; sometimes they are the ones who best know what a good father should look like. God knows how to be a good father.

The Gospel author John writes that those who believe in Jesus are given the right to become a part of the family: "to all who did receive him, to those who believed in his name, he gave the right to become children of God" (John 1:12).

Remember what Jesus called the woman the moment she knelt before him and told her story? He shows her God's fatherly heart by calling her "Daughter."

... He Made You To Know Him As Father Forever

We can only imagine what was running through Jairus's mind as he anxiously waited while Jesus talked to the woman. If only they could get moving again! But as Jesus was still speaking to the woman, Jairus received the blow:

> ... some people came from the house of Jairus, the synagogue leader. "Your daughter is dead," they said. "Why bother the teacher anymore?" (Mark 5:35)

Despite the news, Jesus continued to the house, now filled with the loud wailings of this important man's many friends and family.

> [Jesus] took the child's father and mother and the disciples who were with him, and went in where the child was. He took her by the hand and said to her, "Talitha koum!" (which means "Little girl, I say to you, get up!"). Immediately the girl stood up and began to walk around (she was twelve years old). At this they were completely astonished. (Mark 5:40–42)

With tender compassion, Jesus restored another life and another family. But as Jesus raised this twelve-year-old, he didn't just transform her parents' sorrow to joy; he showed us on a small scale, what he will do on an ultimate scale.

Jesus can give us eternal life—knowing and enjoying our Father God eternally in an ever-maturing relationship. We are deeply valuable to God because we are eternal beings. He created us as infinite beings. Our bodies die, but our spirit will live forever. We matter to God. He made us to spend that forever with him.

LIE 2

BEING GOOD IS GOOD ENOUGH

My father is a physician, an orthopedic surgeon. In his career he has helped thousands of people. But almost every good news story involving my dad begins with bad news. The scene would often go something like this: a patient finds themself in Dad's office only to hear: "I'm afraid it's serious. Your hip is in such bad shape that, left to itself, you won't be able to walk again."

The bad news was always a shock. Then, once it sank in, he offered a solution: "But with surgery, we can replace the hip joint, and you'll be better than new."

That's the shape of good physician care: first bad news, then good. And when presented with the options, no patient chose a wheelchair over surgery.

The same is true for our souls. Jesus is an expert physician with good news for the world. But first …

The Bad News

To be a religious leader in the days of Jesus was to be rich, powerful, and feared. At the top of the ladder of the many religious sects sat the most serious-minded religious group: the Pharisees. They hounded Jesus. Yet Jesus boldly and publicly called them hypocrites and blind guides. Most Pharisees responded to Jesus with hate and plotted to murder him.

But some Pharisees wondered, and one of them, Nicodemus, sought Jesus out.

We don't know his agenda or why he came to Jesus at night. I suspect he came to instruct this unschooled carpenter in public relations. If only Jesus would stop speaking truth to power, he could improve his popularity.

We might wonder if Nicodemus came under the cover of darkness to avoid being seen with Jesus—after all, it would be bad for his reputation. Regardless, Nicodemus saw something in Jesus that made him risk it.

As the two men talked, the one ending up in the classroom was Nicodemus. Jesus once again spoke truth to power, and his diagnosis was serious:

> Now there was a Pharisee, a man named Nicodemus who was a member of the Jewish ruling council. He came to Jesus at night and said, "Rabbi, we know that you are a teacher who has come from God. For no one could perform the signs you are doing if God were not with him."

> Jesus replied, "Very truly I tell you, no one can see the kingdom of God unless they are born again." (John 3:1–3)

Nicodemus was not just religious, he was a political ruler in Israel's capital city, Jerusalem. Yet none of that seemed to matter to Jesus. Whatever position a person might have in the kingdoms of earth, Jesus assured Nicodemus: "no one can see the kingdom of *God* unless they are born again."

Here is the shocking and blunt diagnosis: no one, not even Nicodemus, is fit for heaven. No matter his strict religious observance, impeccable moral behavior, or civic-minded respectability, nothing about Nicodemus's life or character gave him access to God.

Like a good doctor, Jesus doesn't dress the bad news up or skirt round the truth. Nicodemus needed to start again from scratch with Jesus: to be born again. To say that this diagnosis shocked the patient would be an understatement.

> "How can someone be born when they are old?" Nicodemus asked. "Surely they cannot enter a second time into their mother's womb to be born!" (John 3:4)

Nicodemus takes Jesus literally, dismissing his words as absurd. Jesus explains again:

> Jesus answered, "Very truly I tell you, no one can enter the kingdom of God unless they are born of water and the Spirit. Flesh gives birth to flesh, but the Spirit gives birth to spirit. You should not be surprised at my saying, 'You must be born again.'" (John 3:5–7)

The rebirth we need is not physical, but spiritual. Our physical birth gave us physical life but if we want spiritual life, we need spiritual birth. Without it we're spiritually unborn, or to put it more accurately, spiritually dead. And none of our human efforts or goodness or religion can change that.

This is our problem and it's as old as Adam.

An Ancient Problem

There hasn't always been a problem. Let's rewind the biblical story and see where it all went wrong. Nicodemus should have known these truths. Here's what Israel's teacher should have remembered …

There was a time when things were perfect. In the beginning, we once knew our creator God by sight, and made in God's image, Adam and Eve talked to him face to face, and loved him, and each other, and the world. Overflowing with love and joy, God put much of himself into the human race.

Then, inexplicably, our first father and mother rebelled against God and his ways. Though God warned them that disobedience would bring death, Satan, the fallen angel and God-hater, lured them into foolish treachery by giving them the vain hope of becoming gods. Satan lied, of course. But our mother and father committed high treason against their former friend and creator.

Though God loved them, God loved justice, too. His judgment was separation: people would no longer know fellowship with God. The curse brought things previously unknown: hatred, jealousy, murder, ongoing war, separation between people and God, and a death worse than death in an eternal hell.

The curse was passed from generation to generation—flesh gave birth to flesh. We became like crack babies, inheriting the sins of our fathers, born in twitchy rebellion, treason, and sin, always accompanied by an unnatural separation from God. We feel it, this estrangement.

As soon as humanity fell there was alienation between people and the rest of God's creation when the world became less of a garden and more of a wilderness. There was alienation between men and women and in the family; it was not long into human history when brother murdered brother. Worst of all, there was alienation between us and God.

We are flesh and we only produce more flesh. Earthly life only creates more earthly life. What comes naturally is not the life of heaven, it's a life cut off from heaven. We are like branches of a tree severed from our life source, withering and perishing. My dad never had to give anyone news this bad in his doctor's office.

And if this situation wasn't bad enough, a false cure has been doing the rounds ever since—one which billions have signed up for—*being good is good enough*.

But it's a lie.

Being Good Really Isn't Good Enough

Of course, religious Nicodemus knew the Genesis account of humanity's fall. He knew the bad news. The problem was he seemed to have fallen for the false cure too. I can well imagine him saying: "Absolutely, the problem is deep, so we can't just hope for the best, we need to strive to be good! We need to keep all those religious observances!" Giving to charity, going to church, volunteering, social justice. No murder, no stealing, no judging others. Then our good deeds will outweigh our bad deeds and God will give us the nod of approval.

Being good is good enough, surely? This belief in human goodness is popular and deadly, which is why Jesus challenges it so starkly in John chapter 3. He asks us to be honest with ourselves. It's not easy.

I love my wife, children, parents, and good friends. But, honestly, when I think of my deepest regrets—those things I would give my life to take back—I see the hypocrisy of hurting the very people I love the most. Thinking back on certain things I've said and done, I wince at my foolish pride. Mixed up with all that is admirable in each one of us is a whole host of wrong motives and selfish reflexes.

It's often easier to see other people's faults, but I know that the high standards I set for them are impossible for me. I'm very good at being inconsistent. I'm very good at justifying myself. I hate those hypocrisies, but I see them there when I stop trying to make excuses. I suspect you sometimes feel the same, and that, at least, makes two of us.

We struggle on, trying to manage our issues of bad behavior, racism, anger, lust, greed, but it only seems to pop up in other places in our lives. We stuff these sinful behaviors deep, only to have them come out in unhealthy ways. As a result, we often are unaware of the damage we cause to ourselves, or those around us, until it's too late.

But when a secret addiction results in a public hearing in a courtroom, or the death of a loved one surfaces deep regrets, or a cancer diagnosis makes us face our mortality and fears of what comes next—the list is endless—something changes.

When faced with tragedy, death, regrets, or human fragility, that is, when faced with who we are, we see the truth of what Jesus says: "flesh gives birth to flesh." We live out lives of selfishness and frailty, and this earthly life clings to us like skin to our bones. We can't escape it. So cleaning up our act isn't enough. We need rebirth.

Just What the Doctor Ordered

When my father gave a diagnosis, he did not expect his patients to then operate on themselves. He gave the bad news *and* he gave the cure. God is the same.

When Jesus told Nicodemus he needed to be "born again" he held out an ancient hope. It should have reminded Nicodemus of God's promise preached through the Old Testament prophet Ezekiel:

> "I will cleanse you ... I will give you a new heart and put a new spirit within you; I will remove from you your heart of stone and give you a heart of flesh." (Ezekiel 36:25–26)

Notice all the times God says "I." *God* will solve this problem. *God* is the physician offering to perform a spiritual heart surgery.

Ironically, last year my father fell and broke his hip. He would later tell me that he would have had much more sympathy for his patients had it happened before his retirement. But imagine the scene: he is wheeled into the hospital on the gurney, given the instruments used for a total hip replacement and told to operate on himself. That's what many imagine Christianity asks them to do.

The Bible is even more graphic. The description of our natural spiritual condition is that we are dead on arrival (DOA). And there's nothing any of us can do about it. Any emergency room nurse will tell you that DOA patients don't hook themselves to a ventilator, charge the defibrillator, and zap themselves back to life. It always takes the outside work of nurses and doctors to do that.

Likewise, we're spiritually DOA at birth—flesh has only ever given birth to more flesh. We need outside help. We need the Spirit of God to zap us into new life by giving us a new heart that replaces our stone-cold one.

Without this work of God in our hearts, we cannot know him. Jesus was emphatic about this: unless we are born again, we cannot enter, we cannot even *see*, the kingdom of God. So it's not actually about being good. It's about being remade.

All this isn't easy to hear but it comes from Jesus. And he said it to one of the most religious people on the face of the planet. If anyone could please God by their own goodness, it would have been Nicodemus. No doubt Nicodemus was left reeling from this conversation, as we might be now, but we get a hint that in the end Nicodemus accepted not only the diagnosis but the cure.

Much later when Jesus is crucified and religious and non-religious alike abandon or reject him, Nicodemus is one of the few brave enough to side with Jesus rather than the majority. We don't know how long it took for Nicodemus to wrestle with Jesus' words before accepting them, but I can't imagine Nicodemus ever forgot what Jesus said next:

> God so loved the world that he gave his one and only Son, that whoever believes in him shall not perish but have eternal life. (John 3:16)

These words are for us too. For those who realize they cannot bridge the gulf between themselves and God, the good news is that *Jesus* bridges it for you.

LIE 3

JESUS IS AN INSPIRATION

Jesus usually rates pretty highly in people's estimation. He was a good man, a prophet even; an amazing teacher to learn from, an inspiration to humankind. It's a lie. At least, it's a lie if you think that's *all* he was.

The Pharisees knew better than to think Jesus was a good man. They knew better than to think they could just give him the thumbs up and then carry on as before. They knew Jesus' actions and words disrupted everything they stood for. Even the intrigued Pharisee Nicodemus wanted to set Jesus straight.

Jesus was making these religious men deeply disturbed as he declared himself able to forgive people—blasphemy!—to be "the Son of Man" and "Lord even of the Sabbath" (Mark 2:28). These weren't inspirational words, this was heresy. And far from easing off as the pressure mounts, Jesus picks a fight:

> Another time Jesus went into the synagogue, and a man with a shriveled hand was there. Some of them were looking for a reason to accuse Jesus, so they watched him closely to see if he would heal him on the Sabbath. Jesus said to the man with the shriveled hand, "Stand up in front of everyone."
>
> Then Jesus asked them, "Which is lawful on the Sabbath: to do good or to do evil, to save life or to kill?" But they remained silent.
>
> He looked around at them in anger and, deeply distressed at their stubborn hearts, said to the man, "Stretch out your hand." He stretched it out, and his hand was completely restored. (Mark 3:1–5)

We don't know anything else about the man who gets healed, but we know a lot about those looking on with "stubborn hearts."

Pharisees combined politics and a strict interpretation of religious law. In modern terms, they would be like a US congressman or British MP but undergirded with righteous religious practice. They never met a law they didn't like. And they especially liked the ones about keeping the Sabbath—their holy day—so much so they'd supplemented God's commandment to rest for a day each week with details about *exactly* what constituted "work." Even carrying a mat or walking further than three-quarters of a mile were two of the many things out of bounds.

Was it right for Jesus to heal on a Sabbath day? They didn't need to debate for long:

> Then the Pharisees went out and began to plot with the Herodians how they might kill Jesus. (Mark 3:6)

No appreciation for the man's healing. No amazement that Jesus could perform this miracle. No doubts about their doubts. Only one thing: this man had to die.

Jesus knows they will seek to kill him. That's why he asked them if it was wrong to *kill* on the Sabbath. If ever there was a full-blown picture of hypocrisy, here it is: the Pharisees plan to murder—on the Sabbath.

As rigorous as the Pharisees were about the laws of God, they had forgotten that the law was about doing good and saving life, about loving God and loving others. Jesus knew this. He was motivated by more than just love for the man in need of healing.

Jesus could have healed him quietly after the meeting was over, or on any other day of the week, but he wanted to expose the lies of the Pharisees. He saw their hard hearts, anticipated their treachery, and healed the man anyway.

Jesus knows it's as if he has signed his own death warrant. But he does not stop because he knows it's our only hope. This story is bigger than the healing of one man's hand. It is an image of what Jesus came to do.

We are this broken man. We are in desperate need. We long to be made whole. And Jesus gives him more than a new hand. Jesus sacrifices his life to make him complete.

Moreover, Jesus gave his life for the truth to be revealed. From our twenty-first-century viewpoint, we tend to vilify the Pharisees, but just like them, we can stumble over what Jesus teaches about himself.

The Lie: Jesus Is an Inspiration

I lived in Dubai for sixteen years with my family. It's a crossroads of the world with people from all backgrounds living together. There, I formed a friendship with a white South African named Basie. He grew up in South Africa during the days of Apartheid. During those days, Basie believed the white leadership to be right and good. He and his family benefited from Apartheid, and Basie even fought Apartheid's wars in Angola.

But the Basie I knew in Dubai was very different; it was clear he had rejected Apartheid. He loved all people and treated everyone with equal respect. As I probed about his past Basie said something that I have never forgotten: "Mack, you cannot imagine how horrible it was to wake up one day and realize that everything that you have believed, everything you have staked your life on, everything that you lived for is a lie, and Apartheid was a lie."

Could it be that you have believed a lie about Jesus— that you have bought into a system of disbelief that may say some nice things about Jesus, but that allows you to live how you want?

Jesus is far more than mere inspiration; to think that puts you in dangerous Pharisee territory.

The Gospel of John gives us a bit more detail on one of the many Sabbath debates between Jesus and the Pharisees following another healing:

> So, because Jesus was doing these things on the Sabbath, the Jewish leaders began to persecute him. In his defense Jesus said to them, "My Father is always at his work to this very day, and I too am working." For this reason they tried all the more to kill him; not only was he breaking the Sabbath, but he was even calling God his own Father, making himself equal with God. (John 5:16–18)

Gradually, as the Pharisees realized that Jesus was claiming to be equal to God, they had their religious reason to do what they had already decided. Even if they had been pro-Jesus before, to claim to be on the same footing as the Almighty Creator God was unthinkable. They didn't hide their anger.

Far from backing off, however, Jesus piled on the claims. He has the same life and death power as God the Father, he does the divine work of judgment and he demands the same honor:

> Jesus gave them this answer: "... For just as the Father raises the dead and gives them life, even so the Son

> gives life to whom he is pleased to give it. Moreover, the Father judges no one, but has entrusted all judgment to the Son, that all may honor the Son just as they honor the Father. Whoever does not honor the Son does not honor the Father, who sent him." (John 5:19, 21–23)

Jesus believed he was the divine Son of God, sent by God the Father into the world. He taught he wasn't merely a good man or even a God-sent prophet. He declared himself to be so much more than a person to admire or a motivational figure. He's either the Son of God, or he is a liar.

The Truth: Jesus Is the Son of God

We all know people who talk the talk but don't walk the walk. But Jesus never betrayed a friend. Sex, money, power, or acclaim never seduced him. He didn't gossip. He loved the young and the old; he respected rich and poor. He treated women and those of different nationalities with dignity and respect. He never took advantage of anyone for anything. He never made a promise he didn't keep.

When the crowds shouted his praises, Jesus was humble. When the mob shouted for his death, Jesus stood firm. His life perfectly aligned with his teachings and convictions. No mere man could do this. No fake could pull this off.

One of Jesus' favorite titles for himself was "the Son of Man." It's a reference to the Bible book of Daniel in the Old Testament where "one like a son of man" approached God the Father:

> He [the Son of Man] was given authority, glory and sovereign power; all nations and peoples of every language worshiped him. His dominion is an everlasting dominion that will not pass away, and his kingdom is one that will never be destroyed. (Daniel 7:14)

Jesus will one day be seen for who he truly is and worshiped by all. The Son of Man is the Son of God.

We can't take him or leave him. We can't keep him at arm's length by thinking of him as merely a good man or an inspiring moral example. He is the one with all "authority, glory and sovereign power." We need to come to him with our worship as our God.

LIE 4

I'VE GOT TO LOOK OUT FOR NUMBER ONE

James and John lived up to their nickname "The Sons of Thunder." Brash and overconfident, the brothers nonetheless were two of the twelve disciples following Jesus, learning from him and seeing all his miracles.

One thing was becoming increasingly clear to them: Jesus was God's Messiah—God's King, who one day would rule victorious. *Great*, they thought, *we want in on that ...*

> Then James and John, the sons of Zebedee, came to him.
> "Teacher," they said, "we want you to do for us whatever we ask."
>
> "What do you want me to do for you?" he asked.

> They replied, "Let one of us sit at your right and the other at your left in your glory."
>
> "You don't know what you are asking," Jesus said. (Mark 10:35–38)

It wasn't long before the other disciples heard about this private conversation and they were not impressed. *Who do they think they are? Why should they get the best spots? What about us?*

We're told to believe in ourselves. We're told we can do anything if we just go for it. We're told to promote ourselves and prioritize number one. And we do look to get ahead—ahead of others, if we're really honest—in so many areas of life. We want the promotion, the win. We want to be acknowledged and admired among our friends. It grates when others are noticed and we're not.

We're taught to stand on our rights. We make choices which will benefit ourselves. We might not be as brazen as James and John, but we all instinctively want to come out on top in life. The brothers wanted recognition and success; so did the rest of the disciples as they jealously squabbled over rank.

Resentment grew between the friends and harsh words flew, until Jesus called his band of slow-learners together to explain, again, how his way runs counter to the rest of the world:

> Jesus called them together and said, "You know that those who are regarded as rulers of the Gentiles [non-Jews] lord it over them, and their high officials exercise authority over them. Not so with you. Instead, whoever wants to become great among you must be your servant, and whoever wants to be first must be slave of all. For even the Son of Man [Jesus] did not come to be served, but to serve, and to give his life as a ransom for many." (Mark 10:42–45)

Jesus says following him means putting others first. Following Jesus is not the path upward to worldly greatness. It's following Jesus down into service.

And why? Because, that's what Jesus did. Despite being "in very nature God ... he made himself nothing"; he gave up the splendor of heaven and was "made in human likeness" (Philippians 2:6–7). Jesus, fully God, became also fully man.

He could have stayed in heaven and yet he chose to be born to a poor family and lived a hard life, before dying an agonizing death. He became one of us to help us. He put others first. Jesus himself is a servant.

The Way of the Cross

Even before James and John submitted their promotion request, the disciples questioned the wisdom of Jesus. Following Jesus meant traveling to Jerusalem putting them all in grave danger. It meant a showdown with those who had long decided to execute this preacher. Jesus confirms their fears:

> They were on their way up to Jerusalem, with Jesus leading the way, and the disciples were astonished, while those who followed were afraid. Again he took the Twelve aside and told them what was going to happen to him.
>
> "We are going up to Jerusalem," he said, "and the Son of Man will be delivered over to the chief priests and the teachers of the law. They will condemn him to death and will hand him over to the Gentiles, who will mock him and spit on him, flog him and kill him. Three days later he will rise." (Mark 10:32–34)

To be put on a cross was to be tortured to death. Crucifixion took place in public, and those crucified often suffered for days. They died of asphyxiation: each breath required a push up against the nails driven through hands and feet until weakness and pain caused them to drop down again—over and over.

It was a death of humiliation, anguish, and excruciating pain. It's hard to imagine a crueler form of execution, and it served effectively to keep the populace in line.

Yet to die by crucifixion had always been Jesus' plan—decided long before he'd walked on the earth. Jesus refused to put himself first and instead put others way before himself. Which leads to the obvious question: How does dying this terrible death help us? It seems a strange way to serve others.

Remember what Jesus told James and John: "For even the Son of Man [Jesus] did not come to be served, but to serve, and to give his life as a ransom for many." The way Jesus puts others before himself is to die to ransom them.

Kidnapped

Until recently I lived in Iraq. While there, I received a circular from the American Embassy for US citizens living in the country:

Location: *Iraq.* Event: *The Department of State has updated the Travel Advisory for Iraq with information about Civil Unrest:*

Do not travel to Iraq due to terrorism, kidnapping, armed conflict, civil unrest, COVID-19, and Mission Iraq's limited capacity to provide support to U.S. citizens.

Have a nice day.

During my time in Iraq, I often received these sorts of messages but what caught my attention in this more recent circular was the inclusion of "kidnapping." I lived for years in lands where kidnapping was big business.

In 2016, there were over 700 kidnappings in Baghdad, and those are just the ones reported. The value of the person determines the amount paid. For corporate executives, it can be outrageous sums of money. For poor pastors—not so much. One ransom payment, made near where we lived, was perhaps one of the largest ever: half a billion dollars for twenty-six Qatari citizens, some of whom were part of the royal family.

Those twenty-six people were acutely aware of their need to be ransomed, but there are many others in the world who, even though they don't realize it, need someone to ransom them too.

In fact, we all do.

We're Not As Free As We Think

No one can be sure exactly how many enslaved people there were in the Roman Empire, but estimates range in the millions. Some were born into slavery, others captured in war, still others were sold, or even sold themselves, into slavery due to debt. For most, it was a life sentence, but there was, for some, a small hope of freedom. Freedom could be bought.

Rather than putting himself first, Jesus said that he would "give his life as a *ransom* for many," the Greek word used described the payment given to free an enslaved person. I don't know about you, but there was a time when I didn't feel the need to be freed from anything. We can be easily deceived.

On another occasion Jesus explained: "everyone who sins is a slave to sin" (John 8:34).

Most people think racism, murder, or child abuse are sins, and they are undoubtedly correct. But Jesus taught that those sins come from one source: our sinful condition.

We might avoid murdering someone, but who truly could say that they're free of the root cause—anger? I might not steal, but envy and jealousy seem to flow up from my heart spontaneously. So does the desire to deceive, to be greedy, to hate. Like James and John, we are full of self-interest. We instinctively want to look after number one, even when that comes at the expense of others.

We're trapped in sin.

Don't believe me? Try going a day loving everyone you see as you love yourself. James and John couldn't do it and nor can we. We quickly find we're slaves to pride, impatience, selfishness, all sorts of things. Individual sins flow out of us as expressions of our underlying sin condition, like symptoms of a deadly disease. It's one of those rare times in the English language when the plural (sins) is smaller than the singular (sin). And we're enslaved by it.

At its core, our sin condition is unbelief. Unbelief started our separation from God by our ancestors, and continues when we don't believe God today. We don't believe he is a good God who will provide for us, so we fight to get what we need. We don't believe that his ways are the best or that sins hurt our souls. We go our way, putting ourselves first, all because we don't trust him.

And when we reject God, we are left only with his judgment. But that's not our only option.

It Is Paid

We deserve God's judgment and punishment. Like Adam and Eve at the beginning, we deserve to be shut out of God's presence and remain alienated from him forever. But Jesus takes the punishment so we can go free.

Just like an enslaved person in the Roman Empire could be ransomed, so can we from our slavery to sin. On the cross Jesus paid the ransom to free us. This is not a payment we could ever make on our own. Jesus offered his perfect life in exchange for our indebted lives and he did this willingly. This payment sets free all who would come to him.

On the cross, the last words of Jesus before he died were, "It is finished" (John 19:30). You could translate that phrase, "It is paid!" Jesus has delivered the ransom: a perfect life poured out to death. And what is our response? We need to humbly receive that gift. The biblical word is "faith."

Faith—belief and trust—is the key that opens the door to God. Remember that incredible verse from Nicodemus's encounter with Jesus:

> God so loved the world that he gave his one and only Son, that whoever believes in him shall not perish but have eternal life. (John 3:16)

Jesus willingly came to ransom us. When we look at the cross we see that he died for us. Faith is our receiving of the freedom he offers from sin—receiving Jesus. When we see Jesus crying out, "It is paid," we can say "… and that payment is *for me*."

A Bible prophet called Isaiah described the significance of the cross many years before Jesus was born:

> But he was pierced for our transgressions,
>   he was crushed for our iniquities [our sins];
> the punishment that brought us peace was on him,
>   and by his wounds we are healed.
>
> We all, like sheep, have gone astray,
>   each of us has turned to our own way;
> and the LORD has laid on him
>   the iniquity [sins] of us all. (Isaiah 53:5–6)

In humility and trust we need to ask Jesus to ransom us.

It took them a while to get it, but James and John both got to the point of no longer desperately trying to look out for themselves. They let Jesus serve them by paying their ransom, and they found freedom. So can we.

The life of faith is the life of freedom.

LIE 5

I'VE GOT MY TRUTH, YOU'VE GOT YOURS

It's Friday morning, just hours before the execution of Jesus. The religious authorities have finally managed to get Jesus arrested and in their spite and jealousy, they insist the Romans murder him in their famously brutal manner.

Many things angered them about Jesus, but they knew which charge would interest the Romans: Jesus claimed to be king—the king of the Jews. He'd rebelled against Caesar's rule. So Pilate, the Roman governor of the province, interrogated the trouble-maker:

> Pilate ... summoned Jesus and asked him, "Are you the king of the Jews?"

"Is that your own idea," Jesus asked, "or did others talk to you about me?"

"Am I a Jew?" Pilate replied. "Your own people and chief priests handed you over to me. What is it you have done?"

Jesus said, "My kingdom is not of this world. If it were, my servants would fight to prevent my arrest by the Jewish leaders. But now my kingdom is from another place."

"You are a king, then!" said Pilate.

Jesus answered, "You say that I am a king. In fact, the reason I was born and came into the world is to testify to the truth. Everyone on the side of truth listens to me."

"What is truth?" retorted Pilate. (John 18:33–38)

For Pilate, truth was not a fixed reality to which he must adjust. Truth could be ignored, dismissed, or molded into something more convenient. He considered himself to be in charge, even in charge of the facts.

Reality was what he said it was. After all, he was the ruler; the soldiers of Rome came under his command and he'd got the power of life and death over this penniless preacher. Jesus was a condemned man with no defense, money, position, or army.

Pilate held all the aces. This should have been easy, but on that Friday we see Pilate twisting every way, trying to bend the truth to his convenience. He ends up trapped, as do all who manipulate the truth.

Pilate knew that Jesus wasn't stirring up a rebellion against Caesar. He knew it was the religious leaders' self-interest which motivated their accusations and their actions. Pilate could "find no basis for a charge against him" (John 18:38). Despite this, Pilate was thrown into a series of failed negotiations rather than simply acquitting an innocent man.

If only Pilate had believed in truth and right and wrong, things would have been very different. Instead, he stood in stark contrast to the man. Jesus was unwilling to bargain. Jesus came "to testify to the truth," though it cost him his life. Despite Pilate's best efforts, the crowds screaming "Crucify!" wouldn't stop. The religious leadership wouldn't be diverted from their course no matter what political game Pilate tried to play. Rather than accept the truth of the situation and do the right thing, Pilate frantically fought to keep the angry crowds from rioting and the leaders from undermining him by any means he could. Finally, rejecting truth and justice, "Pilate handed [Jesus] over to them to be crucified" (John 19:16).

It's hard to sympathize with Pilate, but I wonder if we're all prone to want the truth to suit us at times, or to ignore it altogether. We're not aiming to destroy lives, of course. But not wanting to dictate what's right and wrong for others, we too might be tempted to ask "What is truth?" Or perhaps even if we have a sense of what's true, it feels much more compassionate and non-judgmental to say *you've got your truth and I've got mine*.

What's true for me shouldn't be forced on others. What's true for you certainly shouldn't be forced on me. Surely?

You've Got Your Truth, I've Got Mine?

Some things in life are matters of taste. Music styles, preferred vacation, film genre. This kind of variety between people is God-given. But we would never bring that attitude into medicine: *Yellow pills just aren't for me; I prefer the look of the blue ones.* We would never take it into engineering: *I know it's a load-bearing wall but I prefer to demolish it.* And we should not bring it into our spiritual lives either: *I know what Jesus says but I prefer to see things like this …*

The truth is not infinitely flexible. There is a way things actually are and however much we'd like to, we cannot wish or force reality away.

When a doctor diagnoses your condition, you can disagree with the X-rays and test results. You are free to tell her "your truth" about how continuing to smoke will be the perfect treatment. You are free to question her credentials, her judgment, her motivations. You can ignore everything she says. But if you do not adjust to reality, you will suffer the consequences.

I know exclusive claims make us uncomfortable but Jesus wasn't afraid of making them. He says:

> "I am the way, and the truth, and the life. No one comes to the father except through me." (John 14:6)

If you want salvation, Jesus says, if you want to be forgiven of your sin and become part of the family of God, there is just one option. Him.

Shortly after declaring himself the only way to God, and just hours before he stood before Pilate, Jesus knelt before his Father in prayer. In anguish, with sweat falling like drops of blood, Jesus pleaded with God not to go to the cross.

> ... he fell to the ground and prayed that if possible the hour might pass from him. "Abba, Father," he said, "everything is possible for you. Take this cup from me. Yet not what I will, but what you will." (Mark 14:35–36)

There was no other way. Only Jesus could ransom people, and it would take dying in their place to pay the fee. At this point, we all have a choice to make. Is Jesus the only way to know God as he claims, or is he lying?

We can accept his words; if we want to know God, we must trust him. Or we reject his words, calling him a liar. Two options—Jesus' truth *or* my truth. We can't both be right.

Truth Has a Name

There are truths in this world that are fixed, no matter how we might *like* things to be. Actions have consequences. There's a grain to the universe; if you go against the grain like Pilate, you will get splinters. Truth matters.

Some think talk like this is to prohibit fun times. Maybe it sounds like that to you? But my goal is to point you to the truth that guarantees maximum joy! There is a way the universe works, but it's not a stark unyielding force. Fundamentally it's *Jesus* that lies at the heart of this world. The same Jesus who stood before Pilate and allowed himself to be led away to execution.

This is his world and he entered it to save it. His purpose was to rescue people, his mission soaked in love for the very people mistreating him. And soaked in love for us too. That means that behind and beneath the physical hard facts of the world there is something even more profound: there is a person who loves you—a truth that has a name, Jesus!

When Jesus calls himself "the truth" it's not an abstract proposition. He says it in the context of being "the way" (that is, the way to God) and "the life" (that is, an abundant life that lasts forever). Jesus is the truth that opens the door to a relationship with God and an eternity that is out of this world.

"What is truth?" It's one of the most important questions you could ever ask, and Pilate addressed it to the person who could answer it best. But this Roman governor never stuck around to hear the response.

He should have. Subsequent events of that Friday give us the most incredible answer. Most fundamentally the truth is that there is a God who will stop at nothing—not even dying on a cross—to love us, to ransom and restore us. This is the truth—not *my* truth or *your* truth but *the* truth.

LIE 6

DEATH IS THE END

The tears began again as Mary made her way quietly to the tomb of Jesus. The dark early morning felt oppressive around her but she couldn't wait any longer to go to the grave.

> Mary Magdalene went to the tomb and saw that the stone had been removed from the entrance. So she came running to Simon Peter and the other disciple, the one Jesus loved, and said, "They have taken the Lord out of the tomb, and we don't know where they have put him!" (John 20:1–2)

Jesus had promised his resurrection, but even his most ardent believers weren't expecting it. On seeing the empty tomb, Mary reacted how you or I would react. *Someone must have taken the body!* Her anguish deepened.

> Now Mary stood outside the tomb crying … she turned around and saw Jesus standing there, but she did not realize that it was Jesus.
>
> He asked her, "Woman, why are you crying? Who is it you are looking for?"
>
> Thinking he was the gardener, she said, "Sir, if you have carried him away, tell me where you have put him, and I will get him." (John 20:11, 14–15)

Even as she encountered the risen Jesus, the truth of the resurrection had yet to outshine the lie she assumed, dead men don't rise. What would awaken her belief? Wonderfully, Jesus did it with a single word:

> Jesus said to her, "Mary."
>
> She turned toward him and cried out in Aramaic, "Rabboni!" (which means "Teacher").
>
> Jesus said, "Do not hold on to me, for I have not yet ascended to the Father. Go instead to my brothers and tell them, 'I am ascending to my Father and your Father, to my God and your God.'"

> Mary Magdalene went to the disciples with the
> news: "I have seen the Lord!" And she told them
> that he had said these things to her. (John 20:16–18)

She didn't find him, he found her. She didn't name him,
he named her. And the worst experience of her life turned
into the best. She flung herself at her Savior.

I don't know if you've ever lost someone you love. I
have. Mary was overcome with emotion as she held on to
her precious teacher. She lost him once, she didn't want to
lose him again. But Jesus told her to go and spread the joy
by letting the disciples know that Jesus had beaten death.

One Thing Makes All the Difference

The long journey to the US from Iraq takes about twenty-
three hours. A few years ago, I sat next to a man from
Scotland on one nine-hour leg of the trip. We were both
bored and had lots of time, so we started talking.

At some point, he asked me what I did.

"I'm a pastor of a church in Iraq," I said.

His eyes got big, and he stared at me, and then, as if he
couldn't help himself, he blurted out: "Why in the world
would anyone want to do that?" Why would anyone want
to live far from friends and family, facing danger, to tell
others about a man from history?

I could have answered that question in many ways, but
I said, "Well, it's because I truly and genuinely believe that
the man, Jesus Christ, rose from the dead."

He stopped, looked at the seat in front of him, and nodded in agreement, "Fair enough."

He got it. It's the answer which makes sense of Christian faith and Christian practice. The resurrection of Jesus is the hinge on which the entire Christian faith hangs. If Jesus rose from the dead, bodily, historically— properly alive again—then the rest of the arguments, proofs, and explanations about Jesus and Christian faith are secondary.

If Jesus rose from the dead, all he said and taught is backed up. If Jesus rose from the dead, his death on the cross to free us from sin worked. If Jesus rose from the dead, death is not the end.

But if Jesus didn't rise from the grave? Then the Christian faith is worse than worthless; it's a sham and a lie and has done more damage than good. The Bible confirms this: "And if Christ has not been raised, our preaching is useless and so is your faith … If the dead are not raised, 'Let us eat and drink, for tomorrow we die'" (1 Corinthians 15:14, 32).

Wouldn't it be wonderful if "Death is the end" is a lie? If we don't just rot? If there's actually life after death? If Jesus walked out of his tomb 2000 years ago, death is not the end.

What's the Evidence?

I recently heard an atheist arguing with a Christian, saying he couldn't believe in Jesus because the people who wrote about him did so on animal skins. "I guess that means we can't believe in the Pythagorean theorem since it was written on animal skins, too," came the debater's reply.

We like to think we're more intelligent and advanced than the ancients but truth is not about the century we live in, or the mode of communication, but about ... truth.

Too often, people dismiss Jesus for the flimsiest reasons. When people do that, I have a hard time taking them seriously. But when someone says, "I don't trust in Jesus because I don't believe he rose from the dead," I can respect that. They understand this is the heart of the issue.

I'm sad for them though as there's overwhelming evidence that Jesus did rise from the dead. Many have spent tremendous amounts of time and thought verifying this and I want to briefly look at five primary reasons why it's a reasonable thing to believe.

1. The Promise of Jesus

The first reason to believe is that Jesus promised he would rise from the dead. We saw one of his multiple predictions earlier: on the road to Jerusalem, Jesus tells his followers what awaits him—mocking, flogging, death and then, three days later, resurrection (Mark 10:34).

If Jesus is who he says he is—the Lord, the Son of God, the King of the kingdom, the way, the truth and the life—then we can trust his words. In fact, if he is those things, it would be surprising if he decomposed in a Jerusalem tomb. Death is no match for God. The divine identity of Jesus and the truth of the resurrection stand or fall together.

2. The Death of Jesus

Jesus died on that Friday. There was no fainting on the cross only to be revived later. Jesus had been horribly tortured. The soldiers, experts on crucifixion and death, saw he was dead.

Still, just to make sure, they thrust a spear into Jesus' side, producing a flow of blood and water (after death, blood separates into plasma and coagulated red blood cells, but they would have had no way of knowing that at the time, the disciple John just describes what he saw in John 19:34). Jesus' death was a very public affair with many eyewitness.

3. The Appearances of Jesus

The religious leaders did all they could to try and destroy Jesus' following. If there was a body to produce to quash reports of his rising, they would have produced it. But there was no body left to display. Instead, after Jesus died he appeared publicly. His disciples spoke with him, ate with him, asked questions of him for weeks before he returned to heaven.

He taught and instructed them when they were together. He showed them the scars of the crucifixion on his hands and feet. But it wasn't just his closest friends who saw him, Jesus appeared to hundreds (1 Corinthians 15:3–8).

4. The Witnesses of Jesus

If people made up the story, why did they have women be the first to witness the resurrection at the tomb? Women in the first century were not even allowed to give testimony in court. If they were writing myths, the authors would not have women testify. But even more compelling: if the writers made up the resurrection, why would they later die for their belief in this? Who would die for a lie?

5. The Victory of Jesus

Finally, the church spread rapidly without armies, money, or political power, against deadly and robust opposition. Success for such a movement is unprecedented historically.

When Christ was buried on that Friday, Christianity was buried with him. His earthly followers were not impressive people. They weren't the influencers of the day who could easily mold society's beliefs. The Jesus movement should have died with Jesus.

But it didn't. It took hold among his followers who truly and genuinely believed that the man, Jesus Christ, rose from the dead. And from there it spread like no other movement on earth ever has. This is next to impossible to explain if Jesus remained in the ground.

I could say much more about this, but I wanted to list these points so that you can see there's no reason to kiss your brains goodbye to believe in the bodily resurrection of Jesus. If you're skeptical, I urge you to dig in and check out the evidence.

But be warned, the more you investigate the resurrection, the more difficult it becomes to dismiss Jesus. Numerous stories exist of people who set out to disprove Jesus and the resurrection but end up convinced enough to become his follower.[1]

Death is the end is a lie. And that's good news.

When I spoke at my mother's funeral about her life and her hope of the resurrection, the only way to get through my eulogy without breaking down was to remember that my mother's dying day was her best day. The thought tempered my sorrow. I knew my mother didn't want to come back to this life. She had stepped into the joy of fellowship with Jesus, the same fellowship that Mary knew.

---

1 See Lee Strobel, *The Case for Christ* (Zondervan, 2016).

LIE 7

EVERYONE GOES TO HEAVEN

Would you like to know the future? Your future job? Your future lover? The direction of the stock market? How about how long you will live? Or what happens when you die?

Jesus gave his most famous sermon to crowds who sat on the side of a hill. It's called the Sermon on the Mount (Matthew 5–7). That one sermon moved the course of history; figures as diverse as Leo Tolstoy, Mahatma Gandhi, and Dr. Martin Luther King Jr. all pointed to that sermon as a guidepost for life.

Jesus ends the Sermon on the Mount with a story about our future: yours and mine.

> "Not everyone who says to me, 'Lord, Lord,' will enter the kingdom of heaven, but only the one who does the will of my Father who is in heaven. Many will say to me on that day, 'Lord, Lord, did we not

> prophesy in your name and in your name drive out demons and in your name perform many miracles?' Then I will tell them plainly, 'I never knew you. Away from me, you evildoers!'" (Matthew 7:21–23)

If we read Jesus' words closely, we see that Jesus tells us the most important things we can know about our future.

First, he promises that when life ends, we will stand before the door of heaven with all those who have died and are waiting to enter. Then Jesus reveals that *he* is the doorkeeper through whom they gain access. Who gets in?

All Roads?

I've heard people say that all religions are just different paths up a mountain meeting at the same spot before God. It doesn't matter if you are a Christian, Muslim, Hindu, or Sikh.

In one sense, there is truth in that. Every person of any faith (or none) will meet up in the end, says Jesus. But— and it's a massive but—many will be turned away from heaven's doors. Everyone goes to heaven is a lie.

Just getting to the mountain top doesn't mean getting in. At the top is *Jesus*. And there are some—there are *many*—Jesus will keep out of his heaven.

If that's not shocking enough, consider the *kind* of people to whom Jesus says "Away from me." They aren't criminals and arms dealers. They are preachers and miracle workers. "Many will say to me [Jesus] on that day, 'Lord, Lord, did we not prophesy in your name and in your name drive out demons and in your name perform many miracles?'" They are the people doing stuff for Jesus. They sound fantastic! And *they* don't get in—did I read that right?!

What's the Problem?

When I first read this passage, my heart sank, and I wondered if there was any hope for me. If *these* guys with this magnificent heavenly resume are out, then who on earth can go to heaven? Where did they go wrong?

Are these people lying about the stuff they did?

No, Jesus doesn't deny that they have done these things.

Are they being disrespectful of Jesus?

No, they call him Lord *twice*, there's a sense of passion for Jesus.

Have they been hiding their faith, ashamed of Jesus?

No, they have prophesied—that is, they have preached in public with the authority and inspiration of God.

Have they been failures?

No, what they've done is spectacular: casting out demons and doing mighty works.

Jesus is clear that what you say isn't enough. A degree in theology isn't enough. Calling Jesus "Lord" isn't enough. Passion isn't enough. Spectacular good works aren't enough. Those crowds listening to Jesus on the hillside must have sat open mouthed.

If Jesus has any credibility for you, his words to those at the gate of heaven should scare you and make you ask: Why, in the end, are they cast away from Jesus' presence? What was their problem—a problem that has such eternal consequences?

Relying on Yourself Won't Get You into Heaven

Simply put, the problem with these people is this: they are religious hypocrites. Despite being the pastors and the preachers, they are Christians in "name only." They have fooled everyone, including themselves. They have fooled everyone, that is, except the one person who can see the heart, Jesus.

What tips us off to their hypocrisy? Look at what they trust to get themselves in to heaven—themselves! They point to their preaching and their spectacular works. They believe in themselves and that their good works will purchase the kingdom.

Of course, whether we claim to follow Jesus like these people or not, we can easily fall into the same deep hole of trusting ourselves to get us into heaven. We might be tempted to name our social activism, volunteer work, love for our families, or general niceness as our passport in. Jesus says, "It doesn't work like that."

To be clear, judgment day is not decided by your good works. To believe it is, is a lie. Any who claim their performance as a ticket to heaven show that they haven't understood salvation and don't have a genuine heartfelt belief in Jesus.

If our eternity is not based on our moral and religious performance, then what is it based on?

Later another crowd sits listening to Jesus. This crowd is a bit more rowdy than the one on the hillside. There's a lot of back and forth with Jesus answering many questions. At one point, someone asks: "What must we do to do the works God requires?" (John 6:28).

The questioner thinks, as so many do, that eternal life is based on our works and good deeds. But Jesus responds by saying, "The work of God is this: to believe in the one he has sent" (John 6:29).

Only Jesus has done enough to deserve heaven, and he's willing to share that with us out of love. Do we know Jesus? That's the critical question. Does he know us? Have we laid down all claims to our own goodness, and instead chosen to trust in his?

The day Jesus was crucified two other men also slowly suffocated to death either side of him. One heaped insults on Jesus, but the other admitted his terrible life and cried out to Jesus for salvation.

Then he said, "Jesus, remember me when you come into your kingdom."

> Jesus answered him, "Truly I tell you, today you will
> be with me in paradise." (Luke 23:42–43)

This dying man couldn't wipe the sweat and blood from his eyes let alone reform his life. There was no opportunity for good works. All he could do was trust in Jesus for his entry into heaven. Jesus will turn many away from those gates, but this criminal gets welcomed in.

Hang On!

Wait a minute, you might well counter, doesn't Jesus say those who do "the will of my Father who is in heaven" make the grade? This is all just contradictory! Surely doing the "will of God" is about living a good life? But no, as Jesus later explains:

> "For my Father's will is that everyone who looks to
> the Son and believes in him shall have eternal life,
> and I will raise them up at the last day." (John 6:40)

The will of God for you is not so much about a spouse, a job, or where to live. Of course, God cares about those things, but it's not the primary concern of the Bible when it speaks about the will of God. Instead, when the Bible speaks of God's will for you, it almost always concerns your relationship with him. Any loving act we do will then flow out of that relationship. It's not what gives us a relationship with God in the first place.

God's will for us is to repent of sin and turn to Jesus in authentic and genuine faith from the heart. That's what the will of God the Father is for your life. And that is how to make sure Jesus knows you, so you don't ever hear the terrible words, "I never knew you. Away from me." That is how to be ready for heaven.

The Coming Day

I mentioned that I have a friendship with the Olympian marathon runner Wesley Korir. Wesley invited our family to come and watch him run in the Chicago marathon. Millions of fans watched as Wesley came in second place. What a thrill.

After the race, I followed Wesley to the various post-race events, press conferences, drug testing, and autograph signing for the throngs of admirers and fans. Every room contained burly men with earpieces and suspicious looks. And each time Wesley would walk past them without hindrance. I, on the other hand, would get their hand on my chest and a threatening glare, until Wesley would turn and say, "It's okay, he's with me."

The good news is that Jesus says, "whoever comes to me I will never drive away" (John 6:37). Those who point to Jesus rather than themselves will hear Jesus say, "Well done, good and faithful servant!" (Matthew 25:23). They will enter eternal life and Jesus will say, she's with me, he's with me, and be spared what Jesus called the "second death" (Revelation 20:6)—hell itself.

Heaven is filled with light and joy. All struggle and heartache, pain and loss will be forever gone. We will live life as it's meant to be lived. All the alienation we experience between people in this life will be gone.

Jesus promises that the best thing of heaven will be that he is there to greet us and live with us. We will feast with him, fully knowing him and being fully known.

Good news indeed.

LIE 8

I CAN'T CHANGE

Tax collectors were despised in Jesus' day. Sell-outs to the occupying Roman forces, they took money from their own people and gave it to the enemy. They were notorious for charging too much and keeping the difference.

Money certainly was everything for the chief tax collector in Jericho, meaning more to him than social acceptance or anything else. Perhaps Zacchaeus would sometimes lie in bed at night wondering about his chosen path, but then turn over with a sigh, knowing there was no going back. Society would never accept him, so he may as well enjoy his wealth.

Money had a tight grip on Zacchaeus's heart and no one, not even Zacchaeus himself, had any hope of easing the hold. There's a lot of truth in the lie "I can't change." When a person has made something their ultimate thing—be that money, sex, or success—all the willpower in the world won't topple that god. Some have obvious addictions which enslave. Others just can't shake that secret vice.

One morning there seemed to be a bit of a buzz outside the office and Zacchaeus caught the name "Jesus" in the excited conversation:

> Jesus entered Jericho and was passing through. A man was there named Zacchaeus; he was a chief tax collector and wealthy. He wanted to see who Jesus was, but because he was short he could not see over the crowd. So he ran ahead and climbed a sycamore-fig tree to see him, since Jesus was coming that way.
>
> When Jesus reached the spot, he looked up and said to him, "Zacchaeus, come down immediately. I must stay at your house today." So he came down at once and welcomed him gladly. (Luke 19:1–6)

Tax collectors were cheats and collaborators, yet the Son of God seeks out this lowlife to hang out with. It understandably doesn't go down well with the crowd:

> All the people saw this and began to mutter, "He has gone to be the guest of a sinner."
>
> But Zacchaeus stood up and said to the Lord, "Look, Lord! Here and now I give half of my possessions

to the poor, and if I have cheated anybody out of anything, I will pay back four times the amount."

Jesus said to him, "Today salvation has come to this house, because this man, too, is a son of Abraham. For the Son of Man [Jesus] came to seek and to save the lost." (Luke 19:7–10)

Zacchaeus knew that without Jesus, "I can't change" is precisely right. Oh, sure we can make minor adjustments for a time. But genuine deep changes in our hearts only happen through the work of Jesus. We are lost in our sin without him. Jesus came to seek and save the lost.

Jesus explained further at another meal with tax collectors: "It is not the healthy who need a doctor, but the sick … I have not come to call the righteous, but sinners" (Matthew 9:12–13). Jesus knows we can't sort our lives or shake off our sins. That's why he came. On my own, I can't change, but Jesus doesn't leave me on my own.

The Truth: Jesus Can Turn My Life Around

My college friend Paul took great delight in packing up as many of his friends as would fit in his ancient VW bug and driving up and down the main street of Chattanooga, Tennessee, fists raised out the windows, shouting out in unison: "Repent!" to shocked pedestrians.

My friend Paul saw repentance as silly puritanism, a religious show of weeping and wailing following a fiery sermon. That's not what repentance is. Repentance is not merely cleaning up our act, getting our life together, or acting nice. There's nothing wrong with that, but it's not what repentance means.

Initially, the word repent was a military marching command that meant "about-face." To stop marching one way and start marching another. That's what it means in a spiritual sense, too. We turn from going our route and go God's way. Repentance and belief are two sides of the same coin. We repent of disbelief and turn to belief.

Josh was a tall, good-looking university student in Dubai. On a weekend retreat with a group of Christians, I gave a clumsy talk about the vast gulf between human sin and the purity of God. Despite my awkward presentation that night, the truth of the talk pierced Josh's heart like a splinter. He tossed and turned in his bed as his past haunted him.

Later he would tell me it was as if God was cataloging his life of sin before his eyes. For the first time, he saw where he blamed others for hurtful things he had done. He saw where he'd justified himself for the pain he had caused others because of his selfishness and where he'd ignored his cruel actions toward others though those things had caused harm.

Finally, he said it was like a weight was crushing him in his bed. He had come to the place of "owning his sin." He saw that it was his sin, not anybody else's, and he could do nothing about it. Finally, the burden was so overwhelming that he rolled out of bed to his knees and asked for forgiveness from Christ.

Josh felt the burden lift; he knew of Christ's love and forgiveness for him. Over the years, I've watched Josh grow into the loving, kind person he is today, but that was not his trajectory until that evening.

Josh repented that night.

The sharp edge of repentance requires us to face up to our sin. Until we do this, its hold over us is as strong as ever. We won't be able to change. The fact is, left to ourselves, we like our sin.

But it's a gift to see sin for its lie. That's because sin will eventually destroy you and those you love. So, repentance starts by seeing that you are a complete mess of sin and crying out from the heart to God for forgiveness. We own our sin and ask for mercy.

But we don't just wallow in self-pity. We go God's way. We stake our life on Jesus being who he says he is and doing what he promises to do.

Trusting our lives to him, knowing that one day we will see our faith become our reality. Faith, most of all, is vital to God. The Bible says that it is impossible to please God without faith (Hebrews 11:6). Our first parents disbelieved God in the garden, now we reject that path and turn in faith and belief back to him.

We don't "claw our way back into favor," not "get religious," not "be prissy and righteous." But we trust in Jesus. Every relationship requires trust. This is the relationship of all relationships. Faith is central.

The amazing thing is *he* begins to change us from the inside out. When we see Jesus for who he is, we start wanting and, with his help, experiencing change. God's Spirit works in us to transform us.

As Jesus' Spirit works in us, God replaces money in the top spot of our lives. Our hearts no longer worship sex but our Savior. We reject success as our ultimate goal; instead knowing him becomes more important. Our hope is no longer in our looks, abilities, or relationships but in Jesus. We no longer call the shots in our life, but trust God to lead us.

Zacchaeus had a dramatic about-turn as he owned his sin of greed and immediately began giving his money away after turning to Jesus. The process will be slower for others, but it will be there.

A Decision Needs to be Made

My Muslim friends are always surprised when I say all genuine Christians are converts. Unlike the Muslim faith, you are not born a Christian. At some point, all Christians make the conscious decision to put their trust in Jesus and follow him as the Lord of their lives. I would explain to them that this move was not from one religion to another but from life to death, from darkness to light. Ultimately, this is God's work in us.

To become a Christian is a big decision and is potentially very costly. Those around you may be unhappy that you've rejected lies they still hold dear. But you'll gain so much more in Jesus than you will ever lose from the world.

Here is a summary of what needs to be believed to become a follower of Jesus:

- Our Creator God is holy, just, and loving. We are his people, made in his image. Yet, though we were once in perfect fellowship with God, we are now cut off from him. That separation of God and his people started with a rebellion by our ancestors.

- At root, the rebellion was our choice not to believe God and our attempt to make ourselves God instead. That treasonous rebellion failed, and the judgment was eternal death. The sin of rebellion passes from generation to generation like a curse: all people inherit sin and judgment. Our sinful nature makes it impossible for anyone to earn their way back to God.

- But even though we cannot buy or earn our way out of the curse, God in his love provided a way of escape back to a loving, forgiven relationship with him. The entire Bible prophesies, records, and explains the coming of a Savior to do that.

- Jesus, who was fully God and fully man, lived on earth as a miracle worker and teacher of God's ways. He lived a perfect life and became the perfect sacrifice to ransom us from the curse of sin and death. Jesus paid the penalty for our sins through his death on the cross. He rose from the grave, conquering death, and proving what he said was true. Through his death, he offers us forgiveness from sin and the right for any who turn to him to become children of God. His children will live forever with him.

- Jesus will never turn anyone away who hears this message of good news and responds. Jesus calls us to turn from an unbelieving lifestyle and the accompanying sin that entangles us and instead to put our complete trust and faith in him alone to rescue us. So, to become a follower of Jesus, we offer our lives to him in faith and commit to following him as Lord throughout our lives.

If you understand these essential points, you know enough to know Jesus. If you believe this, then you are a believer. You might find it helpful to pray a prayer like the following one—it's a personal response to the God who calls you to a personal relationship:

My God and my Father,

I recognize that you are God, and not me. I repent and am sorry for living without you—living as though I was the ruler of my life and not you. Please forgive me for not trusting you. Please forgive me for all my sins. I turn away from my sin and toward you.

Thank you for sending your Son, Jesus, to be my Savior. Thank you for his perfect life and his sacrificial death to pay for my sins. Thank you that he rose again to give me new life. I trust in Jesus for my forgiveness, for my life, and for eternity.

Please fill me with your Holy Spirit and help me to walk with Jesus in obedience to him through this life.

In Jesus' name,

Amen.

The Bible is clear: "If you declare with your mouth, 'Jesus is Lord,' and believe in your heart that God raised Him from the dead, you will be saved" (Romans 10:9). Mirroring Zacchaeus's experience, we too can know that "Today salvation has come to this house."

WALKING IN THE TRUTH

Thousands of people encountered Jesus when he lived in first-century Palestine. They found him to be anything but irrelevant. When they looked at Jesus, they met with God. My hope is that you too have had your own encounter with him as you've read this book.

Coming face to face with Christ can feel uncomfortable as he exposes the lies we thought were truth. But Jesus always works for our good, liberating us from the lies that both bind us and blind us.

> Jesus said "If you hold to my teaching, you are really my disciples. Then you will know the truth, and the truth will set you free." (John 8:31–32)

If you are trusting in Jesus, you are now walking in the truth. But what does following Jesus look like day to day?

Abundant Life

Jesus promises life at its best. He gives us a spiritually vibrant life, not just eternally but also in the here and now. He makes his followers this promise:

> "I have come that they may have life, and have it to the full." (John 10:10)

Life to the full doesn't mean having lots of stuff or living to excess. It doesn't mean being free of pain and suffering—avoid any preachers who tell you that.

Instead, abundant life means embracing a life filled with joy, love, and peace. It's a life full of good choices directed by Jesus, leading to deep contentment and satisfaction. And we certainly need those things right now.

What are the first steps in this abundant life?

Tell Someone

I had an uncle who came to faith while serving abroad in the military. Some missionaries shared the good news of Jesus with him. Afterwards, Uncle Jack prayed for me for many years and was thrilled to hear that I had come to faith.

At the time, it encouraged me to share my news with him, and now I see what an encouragement it was for Uncle Jack too. So, tell another believer you've become a Christian, it'll encourage you both.

Find a Church

Becoming a Christian means becoming part of God's family. It's critical in the life of a Christian to be joined with other believers. You'll come to love the people of Jesus as you follow him together. You'll find they're not perfect. Some Christians can be difficult and cranky. But most are amazing because they are becoming more like Jesus. Perhaps a friend gave you this book, ask them about joining a church.

Read the Bible

Before I was a Christian, the Bible seemed uninteresting, but my tastes changed once I became a believer. Soon after I came to faith, I found a Bible and devoured it. Something that had once seemed dry as dust suddenly burst open, refreshing as an ice-cold drink after a long run in the heat.

I quickly found that God talks directly to us through the pages of Scripture. I got to know Jesus more deeply. I understood more about myself and the world and the Christian life. God speaks relevant truth, comfort, and hope daily as I read his Word.

The Bible is a big book; sometimes it's hard to know where to start. I recommend reading through the four accounts of Jesus' earthly life—Matthew, Mark, Luke, and John. You'll come across all the different encounters with Jesus we've seen in this book, plus many more.

Pray

Prayer is a fantastic gift; it's somewhat awe-inspiring that the God of the universe promises to speak to us in the Bible and listen to us too. So tell Jesus your struggles, worries, and questions, praying from the heart. He doesn't always give us the things we ask for, but he'll always give us what's best.

Share Jesus With Others

Once Jesus healed a man who was born blind. The hostile religious authorities summoned the man. He didn't know the answers to their questions, so he told them, "I don't know. [But] one thing I do know. I was blind, now I see" (John 9:25).

It's similar for us. We may not have all the answers, but we can tell others what Jesus has done for us. Your friends may not understand at first. They may ask questions you can't answer, that's ok, but don't let that stop you sharing all you've experienced with them.

Some may reject you as a friend, as some did me, and it'll be hard. But, in times of rejection, remember that Jesus—the way, the truth and the life—is worth it. He will always stick with you: "surely I am with you always," promises Jesus, "to the very end of the age" (Matthew 28:20). Those rejecting you can't free you from slavery to sin and give you abundant, everlasting life, but Jesus can. He'll never let you down.

Being Good?

Jesus suffered for six hours on the cross. It was an agonizing death. He had two criminals on either side of him being crucified, too. One requested that Jesus would remember him when Jesus came into his kingdom. Jesus promised the thief he would be with him in heaven that very day. The criminal had no good works to show in his life. He only had faith.

Like the criminal on the cross, we come to Jesus by faith and not by earning God's favor. Salvation is a free gift. But does that mean we don't have to do good things for God? Can we just live however we want if we're trusting in Jesus to forgive our sin?

Good works are not the price of your salvation. They are instead the privilege of those who are saved. Now that we belong to Jesus, God fills our lives with wonderful purpose: to love him by loving others. On the other side of the door marked salvation there is a pathway lined with gift-wrapped opportunities to do good from a loving heavenly Father. They are everywhere.

When we become Christians, Jesus sends his Spirit to live within us, transforming us. It doesn't happen all at once, but over time the Spirit changes us to become more like Jesus; more loving and joyful, more full of peace and trust.

It's the Spirit who changes us so we *want* to do the right thing. Every day overflows with Christ-like acts we can perform: generosity, kindness, hospitality, encouragement—the list is endless. Living this way is such a blessing—so much better than the darkness, lies and slavery of the old life. To walk in the truth means living in light and freedom.

It's life in abundance.

Jesus has been my friend, Savior and Lord these last fifty years and I can testify that his words have proved relevant and true in my life: with him I have known the light of life. It's my prayer that you will see through the lies you've heard or believed about Jesus and see him for who he is. He is worthy of your trust, your worship, your whole life. So let's follow him together.

And write me: mackstiles@gmail.com. I love to hear from people and I'll try to write back.

ACKNOWLEDGMENTS

George Bernard Shaw said, "England and America are two countries separated by a common language." Yet this separation has not prevented the two Brits working with me on this book from showing unparalleled grace and mercy to this American. Sheri Newton and Jonathan Pountney have demonstrated that the gospel of Jesus is bigger than our differences, and to them, I am eternally grateful.

10Publishing is the publishing house of **10ofThose**.
It is committed to producing quality Christian resources
that are biblical and accessible.

www.10ofthose.com is our online retail arm selling
thousands of quality books at discounted prices.

For information contact: **info@10ofthose.com**
or check out our website: **www.10ofthose.com**